Words Their Way

CLASSROOM

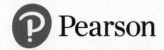
Pearson

Glenview, Illinois   Boston, Massachusetts
Chandler, Arizona   New York, New York

Photographs

Cover ARTIKAL/Shutterstock; eva_mask/Shutterstock; Morphart Creation/Shutterstock; olllikeballoon/Shutterstock; rolandtopor/Shutterstock; Nadezda Barkova/Shutterstock; Gregory Johnston/Alamy Stock Photo

1 (Bat) Getty Images, (Crab) Getty Images, (Frame) Valentin Agapov/Shutterstock, (Game) Tatik22/Shutterstock, (Grass) Stockdisc/Punchstock/Getty Images, (Hat) Heath Doman/Shutterstock, (Map) Digital Wisdom/Getty Images, (Plate) Artur Synenko/Shutterstock, (Snake) Getty Images; 5 (Bride) Thinkstock/Getty Images, (Campfire) Getty Images, (Dive) Photos to Go/Getty Images, (Fish) Eric Isselée/Shutterstock, (Hill) Photos to Go/Getty Images, (Hive) ImageZoo/Alamy Stock Photo, (Kite) D. Hurst/Alamy Stock Photo, (Pie) Brand X Pictures/Thinkstock/Getty Images, (Pig) Anat-oli/Shutterstock, (Prize) Comstock/Thinkstock/Getty Images, (Swim) Getty Images (Twins) John Foxx/Thinkstock/Getty Images; 7 (Kite) D. Hurst/Alamy Stock Photo, (Pig) Anat-oli/Shutterstock; 8 (Kite) D. Hurst/Alamy Stock Photo, (Pig) Anat-oli/Shutterstock; 9 (Boat) ThinkStock/SuperStock, (Bone) Stockbyte/Thinkstock/Getty Images, (Fox) Jeremy Woodhouse/Getty Images, (Goat) Eric Isselée/Shutterstock, (Hive) Corbis/Jupiter Images/Getty Images, (Mop) Stockbyte/Thinkstock/Getty Images, (Road) Alexey Stiop/Shutterstock; 11 (Bone) Stockbyte/Thinkstock/Getty Images; 12 (Bone) Stockbyte/Thinkstock/Getty Images; 13 (Bug) Brand X Pictures/Thinkstock/Getty Images, (Donkey) Getty Images, (Flute) Getty Images, (Moon) Suppakij1017/123RF, (Suit) Karkas/Shutterstock, (Trunk) Getty Images, (Tub) Vladislav Gajic/Shutterstock, (Walnut) M. Unal Ozmen/Shutterstock; 17 (Bell) Jupiter Images/Getty Images, (Jeep) Photos to Go/Getty Images, (Leaf) Corbis, (Queen) Stockbyte/Thinkstock/Getty Images, (Seal) ImageShop/Jupiter Images/Getty Images, (Sheep) Getty Images, (Sleep) Alamy Stock Photo, (Tree) Borislav Gnjidic/Shutterstock; 25 (Kite) D. Hurst/Alamy Stock Photo, (Pig) Anat-oli/Shutterstock; 27 (Kite) D. Hurst/Alamy Stock Photo, (Pig) Anat-oli/Shutterstock; 28 (Kite) D. Hurst/Alamy Stock Photo, (Pig) Anat-oli/Shutterstock; 29 (Bone) Stockbyte/Thinkstock/Getty Images; 31 (Bone) Stockbyte/Thinkstock/Getty Images; 32 (Bone) Stockbyte/Thinkstock/Getty Images.

Pearson Education, Inc. 330 Hudson Street, New York, NY 10013

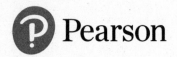

ISBN 13: 978-1-4284-4189-7
ISBN-10:   1-4284-4189-1

1   18

Contents

ă	ā	Oddball

Write two short a vowel words and two long a vowel words on the lines. Then draw a picture to match each word.

ă cat

ā cake

Sort 1: Picture Sort for Short and Long a

Picture Sort for Short and Long i

Oddball	ī		ǐ	

Write two short i vowel words and two long i vowel words on the lines. Then draw a picture to match each word.

ĭ pig	ī kite

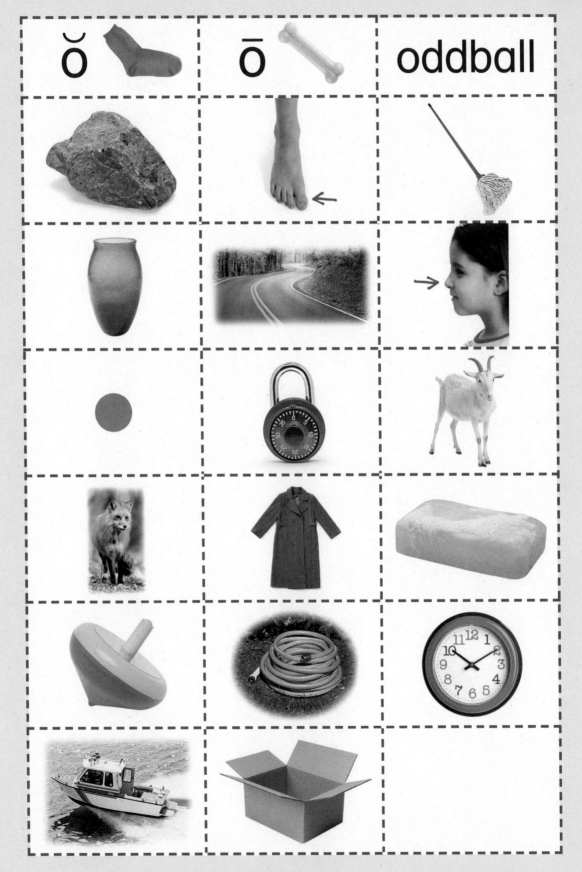

ŏ 🧦	ō 🦴	oddball

Picture Sort for Short and Long o

Oddball				

ō

o

Write two short o vowel words and two long o vowel words on the lines. Then draw a picture to match each word.

Ŏ sock	Ō bone

Sort 3: Picture Sort for Short and Long o

Ŭ	Ū	oddball

Oddball					

ū					

ŭ					

Sort 4: Picture Sort for Short and Long u

(15)

Write two short u vowel words and two long u vowel words on the lines. Then draw a picture to match each word.

Ŭ cup

Ū glue

Sort 4: Picture Sort for Short and Long u

ĕ   ē   oddball

				Oddball

ē

ĕ

Write two short e vowel words and two long e vowel words on the lines. Then draw a picture to match each word.

ĕ bed

ē feet

ă	ā	oddball
glass	whale	bat
gate	make	fast
hand	what	mad
snap	last	page
came	grass	face
base	rake	ask
same	made	sack

ă						ā						Oddball					

Say each short and long vowel. Write on the lines words from the box that have each vowel sound.

last	glass	snap	grass
face	fast	page	mad
same	gate	rake	came

ă — cat

ā — cake

ĭ	ī	oddball
stick	kick	pin
dice	prize	five
gift	hike	life
flip	dish	rich
thin	swim	nice
drive	spill	nine
give	mice	

Oddball					

ī

ĭ

Say each short and long vowel. Write on the lines words from the box that have each vowel sound.

dish	life	rich	thin
kick	gift	drive	flip
prize	nice	hike	five

ĭ pig

ī kite

ŏ	ō	oddball
clock	pot	rope
job	hope	those
rode	hot	hose
joke	home	rock
come	hole	some
spot	chop	stove
broke		

Short o (CVC) and Long o (CVCe)

ō	ŏ	Oddball

Say each short and long vowel. Write on the lines words from the box that have each vowel sound.

rock	job	joke	pot
stove	hose	rope	those
home	hot	spot	chop

Ŏ sock

Ō bone

Ŭ	Ū	oddball
cube	bus	cut
plus	mule	huge
just	drum	jump
hunt	shut	put
cute	tune	such
club	June	rude
flute	use	

Short u (CVC) and Long u (CVCe)

Short u (CVC) and Long u (CVCe)

Oddball					

ū					

ŭ					

Say each short and long vowel. Write on the lines words from the box that have each vowel sound.

drum	bus	cube	rude
huge	hunt	jump	flute
June	just	shut	mule

Ŭ cup

Ū tube

CVC	CVCe	oddball
crop	**note**	
mule	done	wax
rule	skin	safe
crab	wife	lots
cape	tide	gum
have	drip	vote
which	wipe	

Review Short Vowel (CVC) and Long Vowel (CVCe) Patterns

CVC	CVCe	Oddball
crop	**note**	

Say each word. Decide if the word is a short vowel or long vowel word. Write the word on the lines in the box that match the vowel type.

which	drip	cape	wax
safe	gum	crab	rule
wipe	vote	mule	skin

CVC
crop

CVCe
note

Sort 10: Review Short Vowel (CVC) and Long Vowel (CVCe) Patterns

-ck short	-ke long	-k other
kick	**take**	**took**
bike	sick	lock
shook	shake	duck
duke	spoke	pack
strike	cook	lick
sock	smoke	look
truck	like	book

-ck short	-ke long	-k other
kick	take	took

Write on the lines words from your sort that have the final /k/ sound spelled ck, ke, and k.

-ck short	-ke long	-k other

Sort 11: Final /k/ Sound Spelled ck, ke, k

brain	dash	mane
faint	camp	train
stamp	blame	paint
said	snake	crane
snack	want	main
flash	place	snail
bake	black	

Short a (CVC) and Long a (CVCe and CVVC-ai)

ă CVC	ā CVCe	ā CVVC-ai	Oddball
cat	face	rain	

Say each short a and long a word. Write on the lines words from the box that have each vowel sound and pattern.

brain	mane	camp	train	dash	faint
snake	snail	paint	crane	place	blame
flash	black	main	snack	bake	stamp

ă cat	ā face	ā rain

clock	note	stone
none	crop	chose
whole	cross	slope
boat	joke	float
coat	love	shop
lock	toast	soap
knock	toad	

Short o (CVC) and Long o (CVCe and CVVC-oa)

ŏ CVC	ō CVCe	ō CVVC	Oddball
lost	drove	road	

Say each short o and long o word. Write on the lines words from the box that have each vowel sound and pattern.

clock	stone	soap	slope	cross	note
float	whole	crop	toad	chose	toast
shop	lock	joke	knock	coat	boat

Ŏ lost	Ō road	Ō drove

Sort 13: Short o (CVC) and Long o (CVCe and CVVC-oa)

prune	cute	bloom
bump	flute	skunk
tooth	build	trust
grunt	bruise	smooth
built	plus	juice
crude	spoon	mule
suit	cruise	moon

Short u (CVC) and Long u (CVCe and CVVC)

Ŭ CVC	Ū CVCe	Ū UI CVVC	OO CVVC	Oddball
crust	cube	fruit	food	

Say each short u and long u word. Write on the lines words from the box that have each vowel sound.

mule	bloom	cute	cruise
flute	skunk	tooth	trust
suit	grunt	juice	moon

Ŭ crust

_____

- - - - - - - - - -

_____

- - - - - - - - - -

_____

- - - - - - - - - -

_____

Ū cube

_____

- - - - - - - - - -

_____

- - - - - - - - - -

_____

- - - - - - - - - -

_____

U͞i fruit

_____

- - - - - - - - - -

_____

- - - - - - - - - -

_____

- - - - - - - - - -

_____

O͞O food

_____

- - - - - - - - - -

_____

- - - - - - - - - -

_____

- - - - - - - - - -

_____

keep	sweep	vest
next	jeep	team
leaf	when	teeth
sleep	week	heat
west	wheat	been
clean	web	weak
dress		

Short e (CVC) and Long e (CVVC)

ĕ CVC	ē̄e CVVC	ē̄a CVVC	Oddball
less	feet	mean	

Say each short e and long e word. Write on the lines words from the box that have each vowel sound and pattern.

sweep	vest	team	clean	web	heat
next	teeth	west	sleep	keep	dress
when	wheat	jeep	leaf	weak	week

ĕ less	ēe feet	ēa mean

Sort 16

$\overline{ai}$	$\overline{oo}$	$\overline{ee}$	$\overline{ea}$	$\overline{oa}$
throat	beast	zoom	wait	bait
beach	loop	need	scoop	cheek
coast	booth	sheep	train	cheat
seat	goat	grain	wheel	road
neat	three	tail	toast	

ōa						

ēa						

ēe						

ōo						

āi						

Sort 16: Review CVVC Patterns ai, oo, ee, ea, oa (63)

Say each word aloud. Write on the line a word that has the same long vowel spelling. Then draw a picture of the word you wrote.

bait	loop	need
_____	_____	_____

neat	goat
_____	_____

 Sort 16: Review CVVC Patterns ai, oo, ee, ea, oa

Short a (CVC) and Long a
(CVCe, CVVC-ai, and Open Syllable-ay)

past	taste	drain	blame
raise	shape	stand	shade
stray	brain	grain	smash
stay	wade	play	clay
gain	trash	brave	grass
nail	class	tray	gray

Sort 17: Short a (CVC) and Long a (CVCe, CVVC-ai, and Open Syllable-ay)

Short a (CVC) and Long a (CVCe, CVVC-ai, and Open Syllable-ay)

ă CVC	ā CVCe	āi CVVC	āy CVV
glass	trade	rain	lay

Sort 17: Short a (CVC) and Long a (CVCe, CVVC-ai, and Open Syllable-ay)

Say each short a and long a word. Write on the lines words from the box that have each vowel sound and pattern.

play	blame	drain
shade	stand	clay
smash	grain	brain
		past
		shape
		stray

ă CVC
glass

ā CVCe
trade

āi CVVC
rain

āy CVV
lay

Sort 17: Short a (CVC) and Long a (CVCe, CVVC-ai, and Open Syllable-ay)

Long o (CVCe, CVVC-oa, CVV-ow, VCC)

ō CVCe globe	ōa CVVC boat	ōw CVV crow	ō VCC bold	oddball
both	cone	know	throw	cold
blown	told	poll	those	coast
groan	glow	ghost	road	loan
throne	rode	slow	toe	owe

Long o (CVCe, CVVC-oa, CVV-ow, VCC)

$\bar{o}$ CVCe	$\overline{oa}$ CVVC	$\overline{ow}$ CVV	$\bar{o}$ VCC	Oddball
globe	**boat**	**crow**	**bold**	

Say each long vowel word. Write the word in the box that shows the vowel sound and pattern.

| rode | glow | blown | coast | poll | slow | cold | know |
| throne | ghost | told | cone | loan | those | groan | road |

Ō CVCe	ōa CVVC	ōw CVV	Ō VCC
globe	**boat**	**crow**	**bold**

plump	clue	brush
stew	true	knew
sue	blue	glue
sew	do	grew
few	dump	truth
trunk	drew	truck
chew	flue	junk

Short u (CVC) and Long u (Open Syllable -ew and -ue)

ŭ CVC	ēw CVV	ūe CVV	Oddball
thumb	new	due	

Say each short u and long u word. Write on the lines words from the box that have each vowel sound and pattern.

plump	clue	brush	stew	true	knew
flue	chew	sue	blue	glue	grew
few	dump	trunk	drew	truck	junk

ŭ CVC	ēw CVV	ūe CVV
thumb	**new**	**due**
_____	_____	_____
_____	_____	_____
_____	_____	_____
_____	_____	_____
_____	_____	_____
_____	_____	_____

reach	street	head
queen	great	steam
bread	sweet	bead
dream	thread	best
beach	desk	greed
web	breath	sleep
next	sled	threat

ĕ CVC	ĕa CVVC	ēe CVVC	ēa CVVC	Oddball
when	dead	trees	each	

Say each short *e* and long *e* word. Write on the lines words from the box that have each vowel sound.

head	queen	best	bead
desk	dream	street	bread
sleep	reach	next	threat

ĕ when

ĕa dead

ēe trees

ēa each

sigh	bliss	night
try	twice	quit
bright	white	dry
fight	cry	whisk
grill	grim	quite
high	shy	rise
grime	sky	

Short i (CVC) and Long i (CVCe, VCC-igh, and CV Open Syllable-y)

ĭ CVC	ī CVCe	īgh VCC	y=ī CV
quick	write	might	why

Say each short i and long i word. Write on the lines words from the box that have each vowel pattern.

| dry | sigh | bliss | night | try | fight | quite | quit |
| bright | white | cry | whisk | grime | sky | grill | twice |

ĭ CVC	ī CVCe	ī igh VCC	y=ī CV
quick	**write**	**might**	**why**

Patterns and Sounds Spelled with ie and ei

ē CVVC-ie	ī CVV-ie	ā CVVC-ei	Oddball
brief	pie	tie	beige
chief	piece	lie	weight
friend	thief	die	veil
neigh	sleigh	weird	shield
grief	eight		

Oddball	ā CVVC-ei	ī CVV-ie	ē CVVC-ie

Say each word spelled with ei or ie. Write on the lines words from the box that have each vowel sound and spelling pattern.

veil	pie	piece	lie	brief	neigh	thief	die
sleigh	tie	shield	eight	beige	grief	chief	weight

ē CVVC-ie	ī CVV-ie	ā CVVC-ei